Editor
Lorin Klistoff, M.A.

Managing Editor
Karen Goldfluss, M.S. Ed.

Editor-in-Chief
Sharon Coan, M.S. Ed.

Cover Artist
Barb Lorseyedi

Art Manager
Kevin Barnes

Art Director
CJae Froshay

Imaging
Rosa C. See

Product Manager
Phil Garcia

Publisher
Mary D. Smith, M.S. Ed.

Writing & Counting Numbers

Kindergarten

Author

Mary Rosenberg

Teacher Created Resources, Inc.
6421 Industry Way
Westminster, CA 92683
www.teachercreated.com
ISBN: 978-0-7439-8604-5
©2004 Teacher Created Resources, Inc.
Reprinted, 2008
Made in U.S.A.

Table of Contents

Introduction

The old adage "practice makes perfect" can really hold true for your child and his or her education. The more practice and exposure your child has with concepts being taught in school, the more success he or she is likely to find. For many parents, knowing how to help your children can be frustrating because the resources may not be readily available. As a parent it is also difficult to know where to focus your efforts so that the extra practice your child receives at home supports what he or she is learning in school.

This book has been designed to help parents and teachers reinforce basic skills with children. *Practice Makes Perfect: Writing & Counting Numbers* reviews basic math skills for children in kindergarten. The math focus is on counting and writing numbers to thirty with an emphasis on the numbers zero to ten. The following basic objectives are reinforced through practice exercises. These objectives support math standards established on a district, state, or national level. (Refer to the Table of Contents for the specific objectives of each practice page.)

- counting from 0–10 with understanding
- forming numbers correctly
- recognizing "how many" items are in a set
- comparing sets of items to find the set with more or fewer items
- developing an understanding of ordinal numbers to 5
- developing a sense of whole numbers
- representing whole numbers using written form, the number word, and objects

- reading number words from 0 to 10
- developing an understanding of a number and its written form
- introduction to addition
- developing an understanding of "what comes next" and "what's missing"
- developing an understanding of one-to-one correspondence
- developing an understanding of sequential order
- following directions

There are 37 practice pages organized sequentially, so children can build their knowledge from more basic skills to higher-level math skills. (*Note:* For multiple choice responses on practice pages, children can fill in the letter choice or circle the answer.) Following the practice pages are six test practices. These provide children with multiple-choice test items to help prepare them for standardized tests administered in schools. To correct the test pages and the practice pages in this book, use the answer key provided on pages 47 and 48.

How to Make the Most of This Book

Here are some useful ideas for optimizing the practice pages in this book:

- Set aside a specific place in your home to work on the practice pages. Keep it neat and tidy with materials on hand.
- Set up a certain time of day to work on the practice pages. This will establish consistency. Look for times in your day or week that are less hectic and more conducive to practicing skills.
- Keep all practice sessions with your child positive and constructive.
- Help with instructions if necessary. If your child is having difficulty understanding what to do or how to get started, work through the first problem with him or her.
- Review the work your child has done. This serves as reinforcement and provides further practice.
- Allow your child to use whatever writing instruments he or she prefers. For example, colored pencils or magic markers can add variety and pleasure to drill work.
- Pay attention to the areas in which your child has the most difficulty. Provide extra guidance and exercises in those areas. Allowing children to use drawing and manipulatives, such as coins, tiles, game markers, or flash cards, can help them grasp difficult concepts more easily.
- Look for ways to make real-life applications to the skills being reinforced.

Practice 1

Draw a line matching each baseball to one glove.

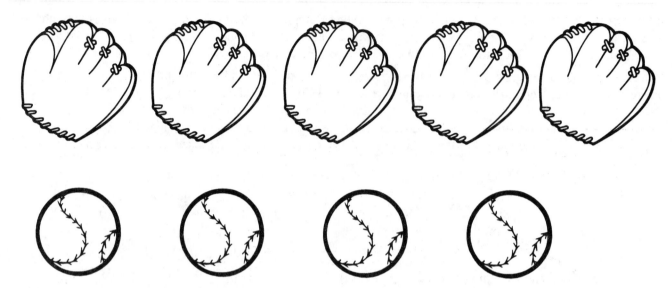

1. How many gloves? _____

2. How many baseballs? _____

Draw a line matching each hoop to one basketball.

3. How many hoops? _____

4. How many basketballs? _____

Practice 2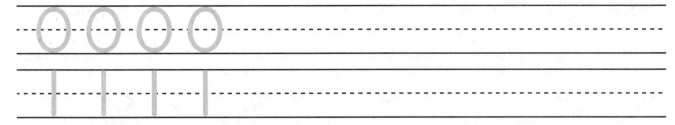

Practice writing the numbers 0 and 1.

Count the items in each pocket. Color the pocket red if there is nothing (0) inside. Color the pocket orange if there is 1 item inside.

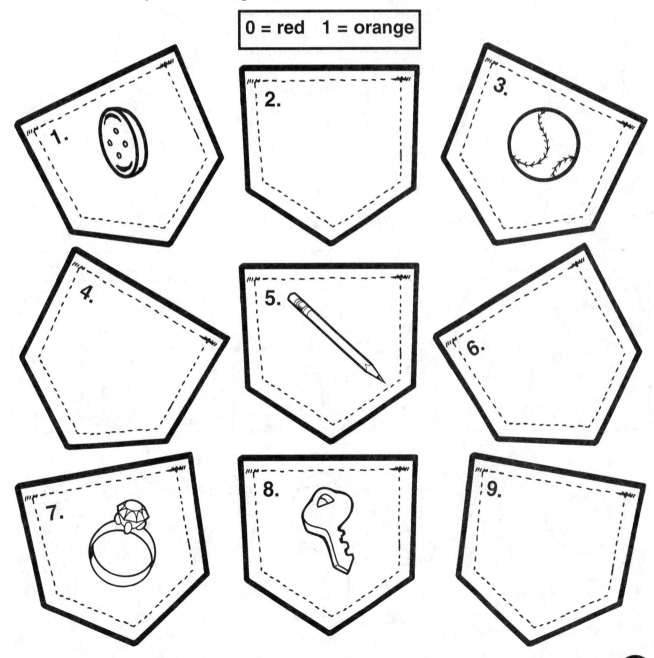

0 = red   1 = orange

Practice 3

Practice writing the numbers 2 and 3.

2 2 2 2

3 3 3 3

Count the peanuts on each elephant. Color the elephant yellow if there are 2 peanuts. Color the elephant brown if there are 3 peanuts.

2 = yellow   3 = brown

Practice 4

Practice writing the numbers 4 and 5.

4 4 4 4

5 5 5 5

Count the fish in each fish bowl. Color the fish bowl green if there are 4 fish.
Color the fish bowl blue if there are 5 fish.

| 4 = green   5 = blue |

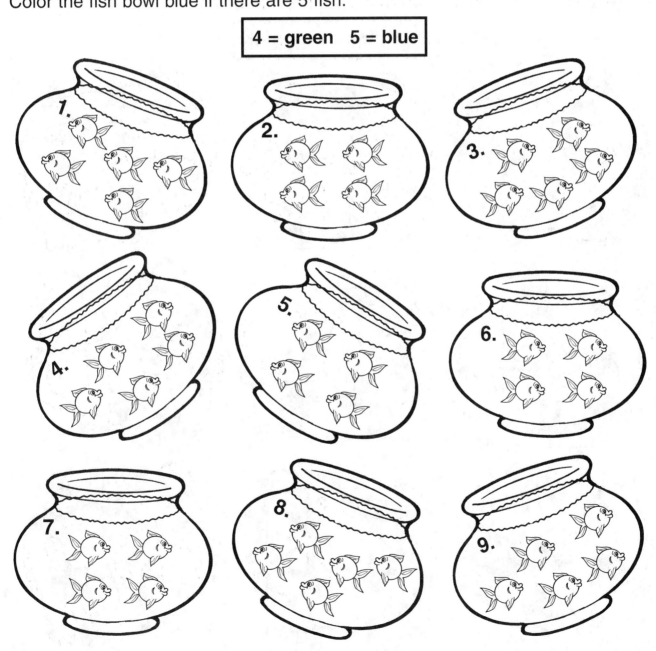

Practice 5

Practice writing the numbers 6 and 7.

6 6 6 6

7 7 7 7

Count the stars on each card. Color the card purple if there are 6 stars. Color the card pink if there are 7 stars.

| 6 = purple   7 = pink |

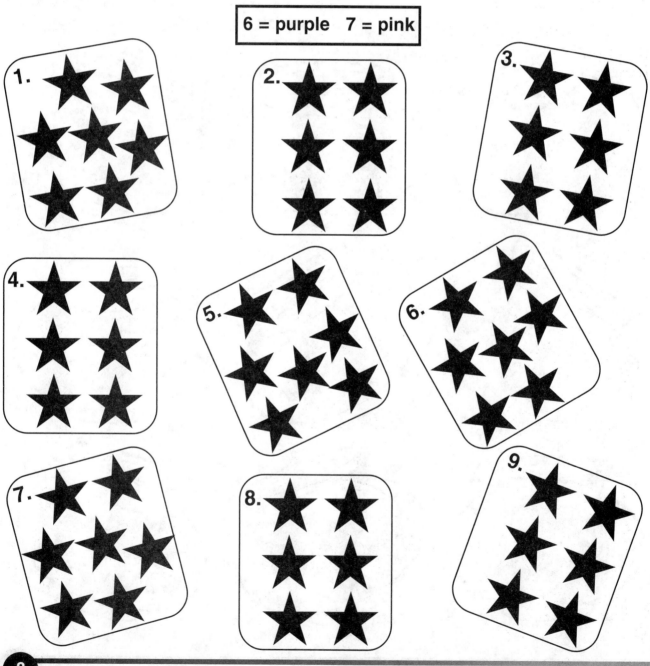

Practice 6

Practice writing the numbers 8, 9, and 10.

Count the pennies in each piggy bank. Color the piggy bank brown if there are 8 pennies. Color the piggy bank red if there are 9 pennies. Color the piggy bank black if there are 10 pennies.

8 = brown   9 = red   10 = black

1.    **2.**    **3.**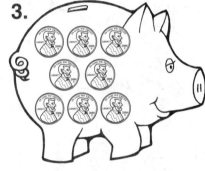

4.    **5.**    **6.**

7.    **8.**    **9.**

Practice 7

Count the cats in each box. Then circle the correct number.

1. 0 1 2	**2.** 0 1 2	**3.** 0 1 2
4. 0 1 2	**5.** 0 1 2	**6.** 0 1 2
7. 0 1 2	**8.** 0 1 2	**9.** 0 1 2
10. 0 1 2	**11.** 0 1 2	**12.** 0 1 2

Practice 8

Count the dogs in each box. Then circle the correct number.

#8604 Practice Makes Perfect: Writing & Counting Numbers

Practice 9

Count the number of mice in each box. Then circle the correct number.

1. 6 7 8	**2.** 6 7 8	**3.** 6 7 8
4. 6 7 8	**5.** 6 7 8	**6.** 6 7 8
7. 6 7 8	**8.** 6 7 8	**9.** 6 7 8
10. 6 7 8	**11.** 6 7 8	**12.** 6 7 8

#8604 *Practice Makes Perfect: Writing & Counting Numbers*

Practice 10

Count the frogs in each box. Then circle the correct number.

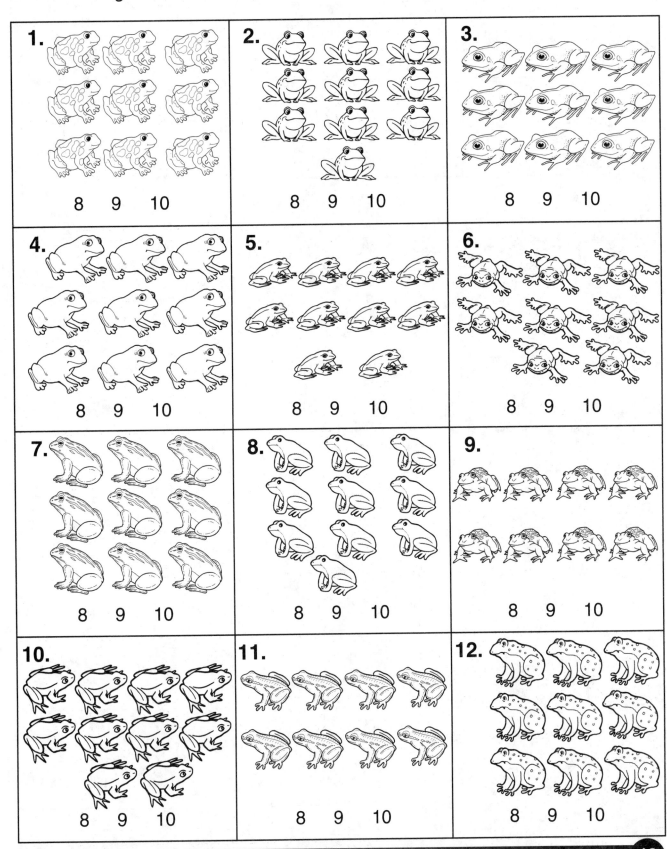

Practice 11

Draw a line matching each set of items to its number.

1.    0

2.    1

3.    2

4.   3

5.    4

6.    5

Draw one more in the box. Write the total number on the line.

7.

8.

 #8604 Practice Makes Perfect: Writing & Counting Numbers   © *Teacher Created Resources, Inc.*

Practice 12

Draw a line matching each set of items to its number.

1.    6

2.   7

3.    8

4.   9

5.   10

6. Make a path by coloring the numbers in order from 0 to 10.

0	10	5	7	8	9	10
1	7	2	6	3	6	8
2	3	4	5	1	9	4

Practice 13

Connect the numbers in order from 0 to 10.

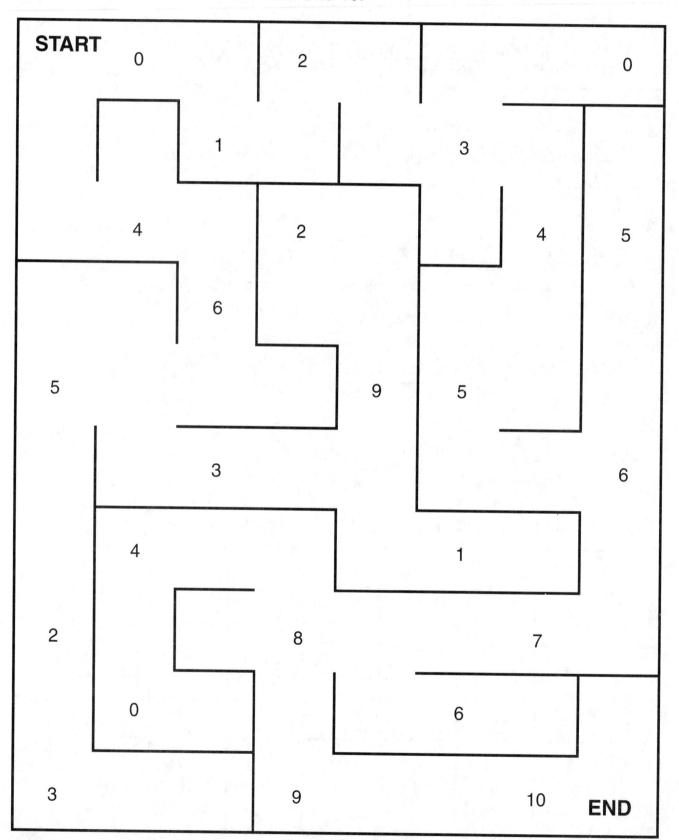

Practice 14

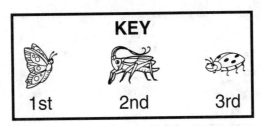

KEY

1st   2nd   3rd

Use the key above to answer the questions. Circle your answers.

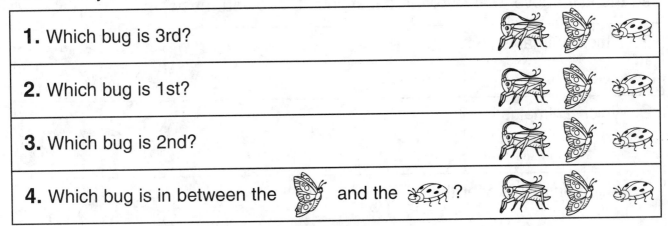

1. Which bug is 3rd?

2. Which bug is 1st?

3. Which bug is 2nd?

4. Which bug is in between the 🦋 and the 🐞?

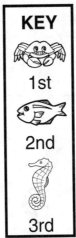

KEY

1st

2nd

3rd

Use they key above to answer the questions. Circle your answer.

5. Which animal is in the middle?

6. Which animal is below the 🐟?

7. Which animal is first?

8. Which animal is last?

#8604 Practice Makes Perfect: Writing & Counting Numbers

Practice 15

KEY

1st	2nd	3rd	4th	5th

Use the key above to answer the questions. Circle your answers.

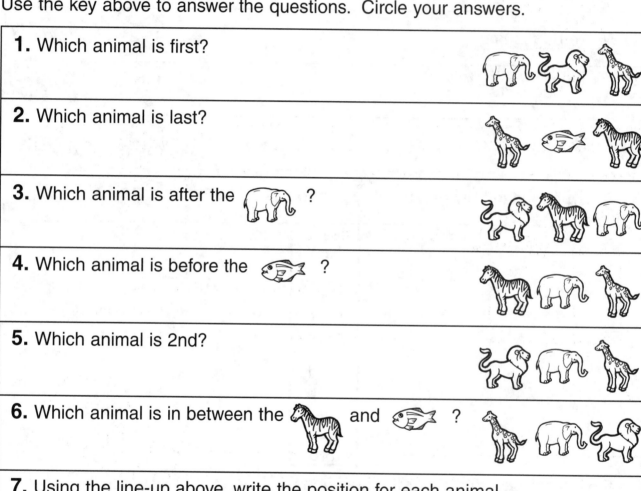

1. Which animal is first?

2. Which animal is last?

3. Which animal is after the 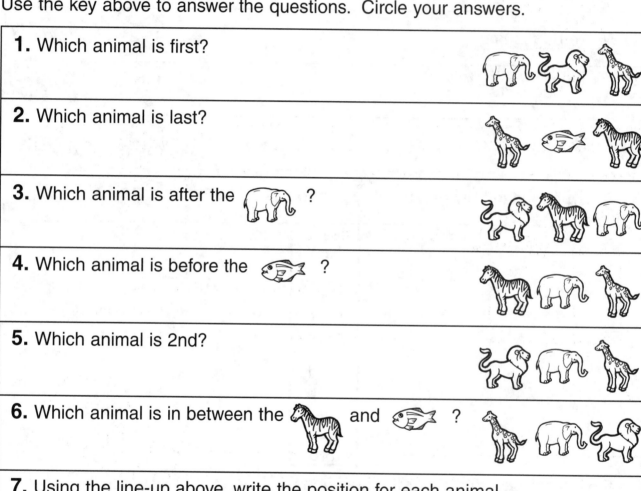 ?

4. Which animal is before the ?

5. Which animal is 2nd?

6. Which animal is in between the and ?

7. Using the line-up above, write the position for each animal.

2nd _____ _____ _____ _____

8. Write the new position for each animal as they are lined up in this box.

_____ 2nd _____ _____ _____

Practice 16

Write the numbers.

1. The numbers on my house or apartment are . . .

_____

- - - - - - - - - - - - - - - - - - -

_____

2. My phone number is . . .

_____

- - - - - - - - - - - - - - - - - - -

_____

3. My birthday is on . . .

_____

- - - - - - - - - - - - - - - - - - -

_____

4. My favorite number is . . .

_____

- - - - - - - - - - - - - - - - - - -

_____

5. I am . . .

_____

- - - - - - - - - - - - - - - - - - -

years old.

Practice 17

0	1	2

Write the number.

1. 	**2.**	**3.**
_____ - - - - - - - - _____	_____ - - - - - - - - _____	_____ - - - - - - - - _____
4.	**5.**	**6.**
_____ - - - - - - - - _____	_____ - - - - - - - - _____	_____ - - - - - - - - _____
7. 	**8.** 	**9.** 
_____ - - - - - - - - _____	_____ - - - - - - - - _____	_____ - - - - - - - - _____

Write the missing number.

10. 0, _____, 2   **11.** _____, 1, 2   **12.** 0, 1, _____

 #8604 Practice Makes Perfect: Writing & Counting Numbers

Practice 18

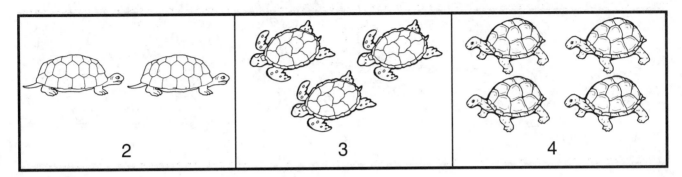

2   3   4

Write the number.

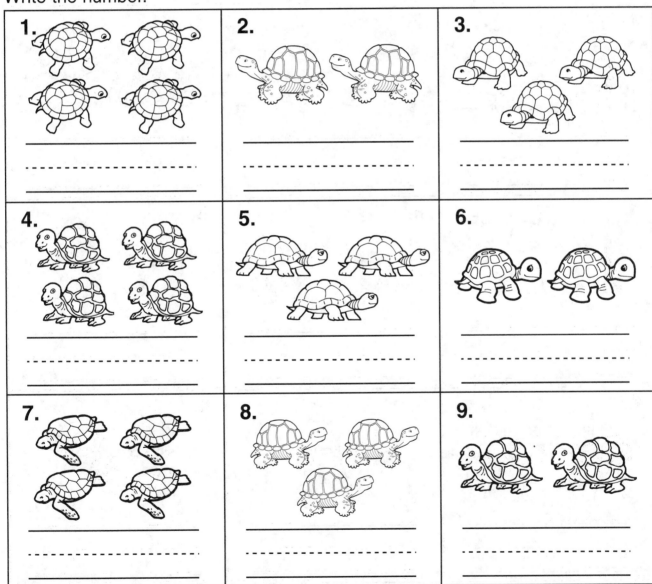

1.

2.

3.

4.

5.

6.

7.

8.

9.

Write the missing number.

10. 0, 1, ___, 3, ___, 5   **11.** 0, 1, ___, ___, 4, 5   **12.** 0, 1, 2, ___, ___, 5

Practice 19

5	6	7

Write the number.

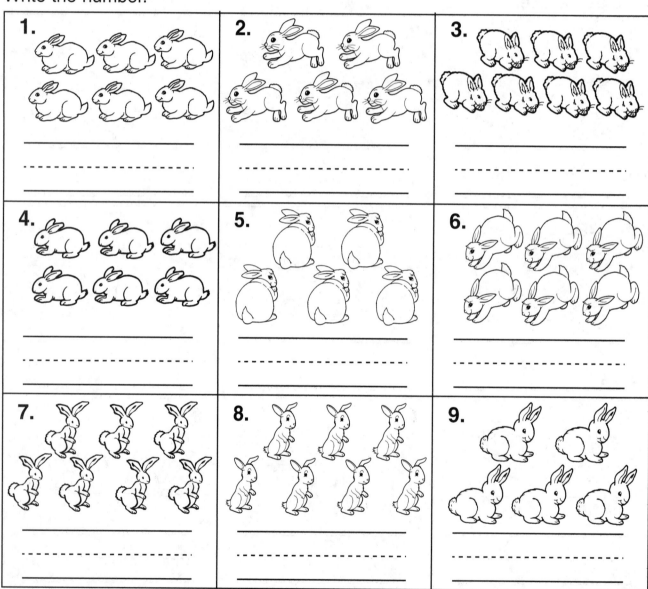

Write the missing number.

10. 4, _____   **11.** 5, _____   **12.** 6, _____

Practice 20

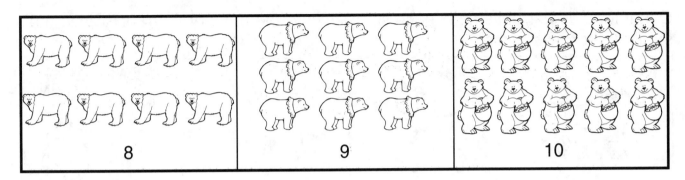

| 8 | 9 | 10 |

Write the number.

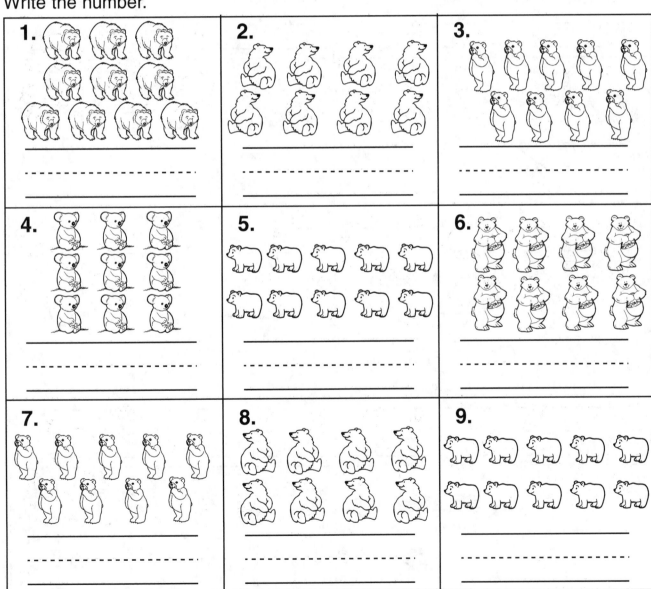

1.

2.

3.

4.

5.

6.

7.

8.

9.

10. Write the missing numbers to ten.

0, 1, ___, 3, 4, ___, 6, ___, ___, 9, ___

Practice 21

Count the number of items in each set and write the number below it. Circle the set that has *more* items.

1.	**2.**
3.	**4.**
5.	**6.**
7.	**8.**

Practice 22

Count the number of items in each set and write the number below it. Circle the set that has *fewer* items.

1.

2.

3.

4.

5.

6.

7.

8.

#8604 Practice Makes Perfect: Writing & Counting Numbers

Practice 23

Count the items. Write the number and the number word.

0	1	2	3	4	5
zero	one	two	three	four	five

1.   5   five

2.

3.

4.

5.

6.

7.

#8604 *Practice Makes Perfect: Writing & Counting Numbers*

Practice 24

Count the items. Write the number and the number word.

6	7	8	9	10
six	seven	eight	nine	ten

1.

8 eight

2.

3.

4.

5.

6.

Practice 25

Draw the correct number of items.

zero 0	one 1	two 2

sun   cloud   star   moon

1. zero suns	**2.** two clouds	**3.** one cloud
4. zero stars	**5.** two stars	**6.** one moon
7. zero clouds	**8.** two moons	**9.** one sun

Practice 26

three	four	five
3	4	5

Follow the directions below. Color the correct number of each item.

- Color four cherries .
- Color three girls .
- Color four boys .

- Color five seeds .
- Color three ants .
- Color five hot dogs .

Practice 27

Trace each number word. Color the correct number of each kind of fruit.

six	seven	eight
6	7	8

1. eight

2. seven

3. six

4. seven

5. eight

6. six

7. eight

8. seven

Practice 28

Trace each number word. Draw the correct number of shapes.

nine 9	ten 10

1. nine ♡	
2. nine △	
3. ten ☐	
4. nine ○	
5. nine ↑	
6. ten ▭	
7. ten ✕	
8. nine +	

Practice 29

Count the number of items in each box. Write the number word in the crossword puzzle.

0	1	2	3
zero	one	two	three

1. ↓

2. →

3. ↓

4. →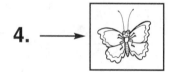

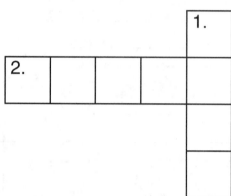

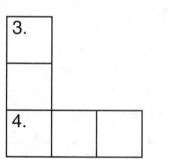

Write each number's word.

5. 3 ___ ___ ___ ___ ___

6. 1 ___ ___ ___

7. 0 ___ ___ ___ ___

8. 2 ___ ___ ___

Look at each pair of numbers. Circle the larger number.

9. 0   1

10. 2   3

11. 3   1

Look at each pair of numbers. Circle the smaller number.

12. 2   0

13. 3   0

14. 1   2

Practice 30

Find and color each word in the word search.

4	5	6	7
four	five	six	seven

four

five

six

seven

S	E	V	E	N
A	F	I	V	E
S	I	X	C	B
D	F	O	U	R

Write each number's word.

1. 7 ___ ___ ___ ___ ___

2. 4 ___ ___ ___ ___

3. 5 ___ ___ ___ ___

4. 6 ___ ___ ___

Write the number word for each set of items.

5.  _____

6.  _____

7.  _____

8. _____

Draw the correct number of apple seeds.

9. five _____

10. seven _____

Practice 31

Draw a line matching each shirt to the matching ball. Write the number word under the ball.

8	9	10
eight	nine	ten

1.

_____
- - - - - - - - - - -
_____

2.

_____
- - - - - - - - - - -
_____

3.

_____
- - - - - - - - - - -
_____

Write the number word that answers each math problem.

4. + _____
- - - - - - - - - - - - - - - - - -
_____

5. + _____
- - - - - - - - - - - - - - - - - -
_____

6.  +  _____
- - - - - - - - - - - - - - - - - -
_____

7. Write the numbers 0 to 10.

____, ____, ____, ____, ____, ____, ____, ____, ____, ____, ____

Practice 32

1. Trace the numbers 0 to 20.

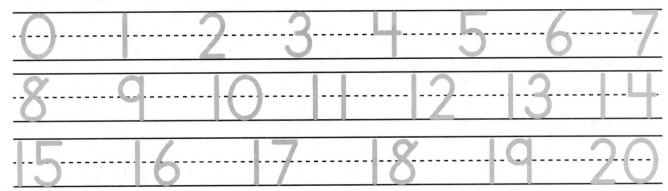

Write the missing numbers.

2. 0, 1, _____, 3, _____, 5, _____, 7, _____, 9, _____, 11, _____, 13, _____, 15, _____, 17, _____, 19, _____

3. 0, _____, 2, _____, 4, _____, 6, _____, 8, _____, 10, _____, 12, _____, 14, _____, 16, _____, 18, _____, 20

4. Write the numbers from 0 to 20.

5. Connect the dots in order from 0 to 20.

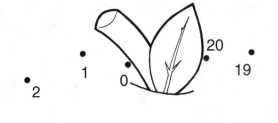

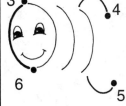

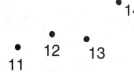

Practice 33

Count the pennies and write the number.

1. _____ ¢

2. _____ ¢

3. _____ ¢

4. _____ ¢

5. _____ ¢

6. _____ ¢

7. _____ ¢

8. _____ ¢

#8604 Practice Makes Perfect: Writing & Counting Numbers   © *Teacher Created Resources, Inc.*

Practice 34

Trace the numbers.

0 1 2 3 4 5 6 7 8 9

10 11 12 13 14 15 16 17

18 19 20 21 22 23 24

25 26 27

28 29 30

Connect the dots
from 0 to 30.

Practice 35

Connect the numbers in order from 0 to 30.

6	10	**START**	20	11	12	13	2
2	1	0	26	10	7	14	11
3	14	19	4	9	14	15	27
4	5	6	7	8	21	16	17
13	13	4	26	9	1	25	18
20	25	24	23	22	21	20	19
12	26	29	2	21	24	22	8
30	27	28	29	30	10	3	3
17	3	9	15	**END**	16	23	1

Practice 36

Practice writing the numbers from 1 to 30.

1.

1	2	3	4		6	7	8	9	
11		13	14	15		17	18	19	20
21	22		24	25	26	27		29	30

2.

1	2		4	5		7	8		10
11		13	14		16	17		19	20
	22	23		25	26		28	29	

3.

1		3		5		7		9	
11		13		15		17		19	
21		23		25		27		29	

4.

			5					10
			15					20
			25					30

Practice 37

Complete the calendar for the current month.

Name of the Month: _____   Year: _____

Sunday	Monday	Tuesday	Wednesday	Thursday	Friday	Saturday

Test Practice 1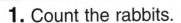

Fill in the circle under the correct answer.

1. Count the rabbits.

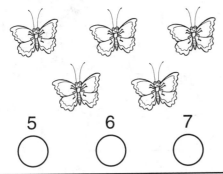

1	2	3
○	○	○

2. Count the birds.

5	6	7
○	○	○

3. Count the butterflies.

5	6	7
○	○	○

4. Count the frogs.

0	1	2
○	○	○

5. Count the bees.

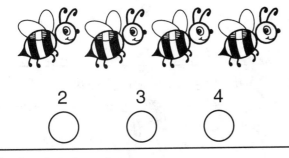

2	3	4
○	○	○

6. Count the mice.

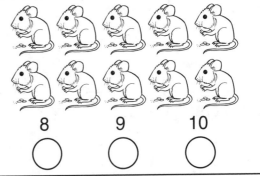

8	9	10
○	○	○

7. Count the dogs.

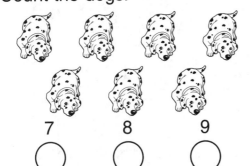

7	8	9
○	○	○

8. Count the ladybugs.

0	1	2
○	○	○

#8604 Practice Makes Perfect: Writing & Counting Numbers

Test Practice 2

Fill in the circle under the correct answer.

1. Which set shows the number 5?

○   ○

2. Which set shows the number 9?

○   ○

3. Which set shows the number 0?

○   ○

4. Which set shows the number 2?

○   ○

5. What number is missing?

0, 1, _____

2   3   4
○   ○   ○

6. What number is missing?

7, _____, 9

8   9   10
○   ○   ○

7. What number comes next?

5, _____

4   6   5
○   ○   ○

8. Count the number of snails.

10   9   8
○   ○   ○

9. What number comes next?

2, _____

0   1   3
○   ○   ○

Test Practice 3

Fill in the circle under the correct answer.

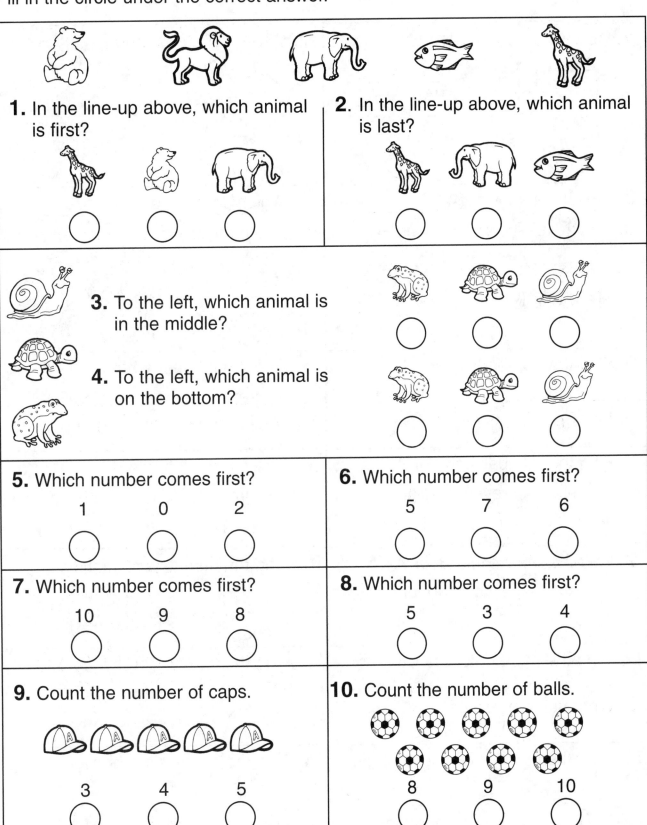

1. In the line-up above, which animal is first?

2. In the line-up above, which animal is last?

3. To the left, which animal is in the middle?

4. To the left, which animal is on the bottom?

5. Which number comes first?

1   0   2

6. Which number comes first?

5   7   6

7. Which number comes first?

10   9   8

8. Which number comes first?

5   3   4

9. Count the number of caps.

3   4   5

10. Count the number of balls.

8   9   10

Test Practice 4

Fill in the circle under the correct answer.

1. Which set shows more?

◯ ◯

2. Which set shows more?

◯ ◯

3. Which set shows fewer?

◯ ◯

4. Which set shows fewer?

◯ ◯

5. Find the number word for 2.

zero	one	two
◯	◯	◯

6. Find the number word for 0.

zero	one	two
◯	◯	◯

7. Find the number word for 8.

six	seven	eight
◯	◯	◯

8. Find the number word for 4.

three	four	five
◯	◯	◯

9. Find the number word for 7.

six	seven	eight
◯	◯	◯

10. Find the number word for 1.

zero	one	two
◯	◯	◯

11. Find the number for the word <u>six</u>.

6	5	4
◯	◯	◯

12. Find the number for the word <u>three</u>.

2	3	4
◯	◯	◯

13. Find the number for the word <u>nine</u>.

7	8	9
◯	◯	◯

14. Find the number for the word <u>five</u>.

6	5	4
◯	◯	◯

Test Practice 5

Fill in the circle under the correct answer.

1. Which set shows <u>zero</u> suns?

○   ○

2. Which set shows <u>seven</u> moons?

○   ○

3. Which set shows <u>two</u> clouds?

○   ○

4. Which set shows <u>one</u> star?

○   ○

5. Count the triangles

six	seven	eight
○	○	○

6. Count the circles.

four	five	six
○	○	○

7. Count the squares.

four	five	six
○	○	○

8. Count the hearts.

four	five	six
○	○	○

9. Find the missing number.

4, ____, 6

4	5	6
○	○	○

10. Find the missing number.

3, 4, ____

4	5	6
○	○	○

Test Practice 6

Fill in the circle under the correct answer.

1. Which set shows <u>eight</u> spoons?

○   ○

2. Which set shows <u>ten</u> pans?

○   ○

3. Which set shows <u>nine</u> fires?

○   ○

4. Which set shows <u>eight</u> flashlights?

○   ○

5. Count the cabins.

eight   nine   ten
○   ○   ○

6. Count the fish.

eight   nine   ten
○   ○   ○

7. Find the missing number.

10, ___, 12

11   12   13
○   ○   ○

8. Find the missing number.

13, 14, ___

14   15   16
○   ○   ○

9. Find the missing number.

16, ___, 18

15   17   19
○   ○   ○

10. Find the missing number.

18, 19, ___

10   20   30
○   ○   ○

11. Find the missing number.

22, 23, ___

24   14   25
○   ○   ○

12. Find the missing number.

28, 29, ___

10   20   30
○   ○   ○

Answer Key

Page 4
Check to make sure the gloves have been matched to a baseball. One glove will not have a match.
1. 5
2. 4

Check to make sure each hoop has been matched to a basketball. Two basketballs will not have a match.
3. 3
4. 5

Page 5
1. orange
2. red
3. orange
4. red
5. orange
6. red
7. orange
8. orange
9. red

Page 6
1. yellow
2. brown
3. brown
4. brown
5. yellow
6. yellow
7. brown
8. yellow
9. brown

Page 7
1. blue
2. green
3. blue
4. blue
5. green
6. green
7. green
8. blue
9. blue

Page 8
1. pink
2. purple
3. purple
4. purple
5. pink
6. pink
7. pink
8. purple
9. purple

Page 9
1. black
2. red
3. brown
4. red
5. brown
6. black
7. brown
8. black
9. red

Page 10
1. 1
2. 0
3. 2
4. 2
5. 2
6. 1
7. 0
8. 1
9. 2
10. 1
11. 0
12. 2

Page 11
1. 3
2. 4
3. 5
4. 5
5. 4
6. 3
7. 4
8. 3
9. 5
10. 5
11. 4
12. 3

Page 12
1. 6
2. 7
3. 6
4. 8
5. 8
6. 7
7. 7
8. 8
9. 6
10. 7
11. 6
12. 8

Page 13
1. 9
2. 10
3. 9
4. 9
5. 10
6. 8
7. 9
8. 10
9. 8
10. 10
11. 8
12. 9

Page 14
1. 3
2. 1
3. 4
4. 0
5. 5
6. 2
7. 4
8. 6

Page 15
1. 8
2. 6
3. 9
4. 10
5. 7
6.

Page 16
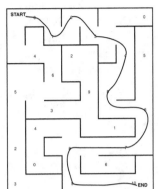

Page 17
1. ladybug
2. butterfly
3. grasshopper
4. grasshopper
5. fish
6. seahorse
7. crab
8. seahorse

Page 18
1. elephant
2. fish
3. lion
4. giraffe
5. lion
6. giraffe
7. 2nd, 5th, 4th, 1st, 3rd
8. 1st, 2nd, 3rd, 4th, 5th

Page 19
All answers will vary.

Page 20
1. 2
2. 0
3. 1
4. 0
5. 2
6. 0
7. 2
8. 1
9. 1
10. 1
11. 0
12. 2

Page 21
1. 4
2. 2
3. 3
4. 4
5. 3
6. 2
7. 4
8. 3
9. 2
10. 2, 4
11. 2, 3
12. 3, 4

Page 22
1. 6
2. 5
3. 7
4. 6
5. 5
6. 6
7. 7
8. 7
9. 5
10. 5
11. 6
12. 7

Page 23
1. 10
2. 8
3. 9
4. 9
5. 10
6. 8
7. 9
8. 8
9. 10
10. 2, 5, 7, 8, 10

Page 24
1. 1, 2 (circle the tents)
2. 4, 3 (circle the nets)
3. 4, 6 (circle the flashlights)
4. 6, 3 (circle the campfires)
5. 2, 4 (circle the barrels)
6. 1, 3 (circle the spoons)
7. 0, 5 (circle the fish)
8. 5, 6 (circle the cans of worms)

Page 25
1. 3, 5 (circle the golf balls)
2. 6, 0 (circle the area with nothing in it)
3. 5, 4 (circle the goggles)
4. 6, 1 (circle the baseball)
5. 4, 1 (circle the net)
6. 2, 5 (circle the baseball caps)
7. 1, 2 (circle the basketball)
8. 5, 6 (circle the helmets)

Page 26
1. 5 five
2. 4 four
3. 1 one
4. 3 three
5. 2 two
6. 0 zero
7. 5 five

Answer Key

Page 27
1. 8 eight
2. 9 nine
3. 7 seven
4. 6 six
5. 10 ten
6. 8 eight

Page 28
The specified boxes have the following drawings:
1. The box is empty.
2. two clouds
3. one cloud
4. The box is empty.
5. two stars
6. one moon
7. The box is empty.
8. two moons
9. one sun

Page 29
The following items should be colored: 4 cherries, 3 girls, 4 boys, 5 seeds, 3 ants, and 5 hot dogs.

Page 30
1. Check to see that 8 bananas were colored.
2. Check to see that 7 oranges were colored.
3. Check to see that 6 apples were colored.
4. Check to see that 7 watermelons were colored.
5. Check to see that 8 peaches were colored.
6. Check to see that 6 pears were colored.
7. Check to see that 8 strawberries were colored.
8. Check to see that 7 pineapples were colored.

Page 31
1. Check to see if 9 hearts were drawn.
2. Check to see if 9 triangles were drawn.
3. Check to see if 10 squares were drawn.
4. Check to see if 9 circles were drawn.
5. Check to see if 9 arrows were drawn.
6. Check to see if 10 rectangles were drawn.
7. Check to see if 10 X marks were drawn.
8. Check to see if 9 plus signs were drawn.

Page 32
1. zero
2. three
3. two
4. one
5. three
6. one
7. zero
8. two
9. 1
10. 3
11. 3
12. 0
13. 0
14. 1

Page 33

1. seven
2. four
3. five
4. six
5. six
6. four
7. seven
8. five
9. Check to see if five apple seeds were drawn.
10. Check to see if seven apple seeds were drawn.

Page 34
1. Matched to ball with eight stars, eight
2. Matched to ball with nine triangles, nine
3. Matched to ball with ten hearts, ten
4. nine
5. eight
6. ten
7. 0, 1, 2, 3, 4, 5, 6, 7, 8, 9, 10

Page 35
1. Check to make sure the numbers were traced.
2. 2, 4, 6, 8, 10, 12, 14, 16, 18, 20
3. 1, 3, 5, 7, 9, 11, 13, 15, 17, 19

4. Check to make sure the numbers were written in correct order from 0 to 20.

5.

Page 36
1. 15
2. 12
3. 17
4. 14
5. 18
6. 16
7. 11
8. 20

Page 37
Check to make sure the numbers were traced.

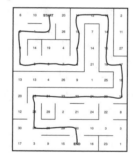

Page 38

Page 39
1. 5, 10, 12, 16, 23, 28
2. 3, 6, 9, 12, 15, 18, 21, 24, 27, 30
3. 2, 4, 6, 8, 10, 12, 14, 16, 18, 20, 22, 24, 26, 28, 30
4. 1, 2, 3, 4, 6, 7, 8, 9, 11, 12, 13, 14, 16, 17, 18, 19, 21, 22, 23, 24, 26, 27, 28, 29

Page 40
Calendars will vary.

Page 41
1. 3
2. 6
3. 5
4. 1
5. 4
6. 10
7. 7
8. 2

Page 42
1. 5 cats
2. 9 crabs
3. space with nothing
4. 2 turtles
5. 2
6. 8
7. 6
8. 10
9. 3

Page 43
1. bear
2. giraffe
3. turtle
4. frog
5. 0
6. 5
7. 8
8. 3
9. 5
10. 9

Page 44
1. 3 TVs
2. 5 pencils
3. 4 lamps
4. space with nothing
5. two
6. zero
7. eight
8. four
9. seven
10. one
11. 6
12. 3
13. 9
14. 5

Page 45
1. space with nothing
2. set with seven moons
3. set with two clouds
4. set with one star
5. seven
6. six
7. five
8. four
9. 5
10. 5

Page 46
1. set with 8 spoons
2. set with 10 pans
3. set with 9 fires
4. set with 8 flashlights
5. ten
6. eight
7. 11
8. 15
9. 17
10. 20
11. 24
12. 30